SCHOLASTIC

Let's Find Out

My REBUS Reader

Hello, Baby Caterpillar!

by Pamela Chanko

SCHOLASTIC INC.
New York Toronto London Auckland Sydney New Delhi Hong Kong

A caterpillar can look like a  snake.

Is a caterpillar a baby snake? **No.**

A caterpillar can look like a  .

lizard

Is a caterpillar a baby lizard? **No.**

A caterpillar can look like a  hedgehog.

Is a caterpillar a baby hedgehog? **No.**

A caterpillar can look like a  .

bunny

Is a caterpillar a baby bunny? **No.**

A caterpillar does **not** look like a  .

butterfly

Is a caterpillar a baby butterfly?

Yes! A caterpillar changes into a  butterfly !

BIG WORD metamorphosis

Caterpillars change into butterflies. This change is called a metamorphosis.

A caterpillar hatches from an egg.

The caterpillar eats leaves.

Its skin hardens into a chrysalis.

A butterfly comes out of the chrysalis.